# PULL-OUT PERFORATED PAGES

# DOT-TO-DOT

# NATURE SCENES

TEST YOUR BRAIN AND DE-STRESS WITH PUZZLE SOLVING AND COLORING

## PaRragon

Bath · New York · Cologne · Melbourne · Delhi
Hong Kong · Shenzhen · Singapore

This edition published by Parragon Books Ltd in 2017

Parragon Inc.
440 Park Avenue South, 13th Floor
New York, NY 10016
www.parragon.com

Puzzles created by Any Puzzle Media Ltd

ISBN 978-1-4748-5865-6

Printed in China

# HOW TO USE THIS BOOK

If you love an engrossing puzzle and are partial to the natural world, here is the perfect challenge. As you move from page to page, you can trace the complex patterns of a leaf, forge a powerful bird in flight, create the complex rhythms of a crashing wave, or outline the delicate filigree of a spider web.

For each puzzle, just join the dots in numerical order to reveal an animal, insect, or natural scene. The first and last numbers are slightly larger, in bold, and underlined to help you find the start and be sure when you're finished. The puzzles are arranged in order of complexity, and they will take anywhere from 20 minutes up to a couple of evenings to complete. By the time you get to the end of the book, you will find puzzles with more than 1,200 dots.

The numbers are exactly centered above or to the side of a dot, or touching at one of the four main diagonals to it, so you can always be certain which dot belongs to which number.

We recommend solving these puzzles using a very sharp pencil so that you do not obscure unused dots and numbers. A ruler can be used to draw the lines, if preferred, but this is not essential. You will find that sometimes it is necessary to go over lines that you have already drawn. If you make a mistake, then just carry on because the line-art nature of each picture is very forgiving.

Once you've joined all the dots, you can color in the resulting image. The perforations along each page allow you to tear out any puzzle, so you could give these to friends or even put them on your wall.

The back pages of the book provide a small preview of each completed image, so avoid looking at these in advance if you don't want to ruin the challenge of doing the puzzles!

Dot to dot has never been more challenging …

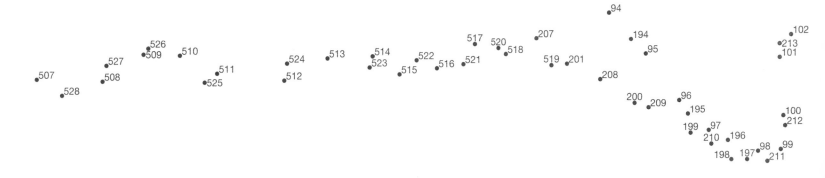

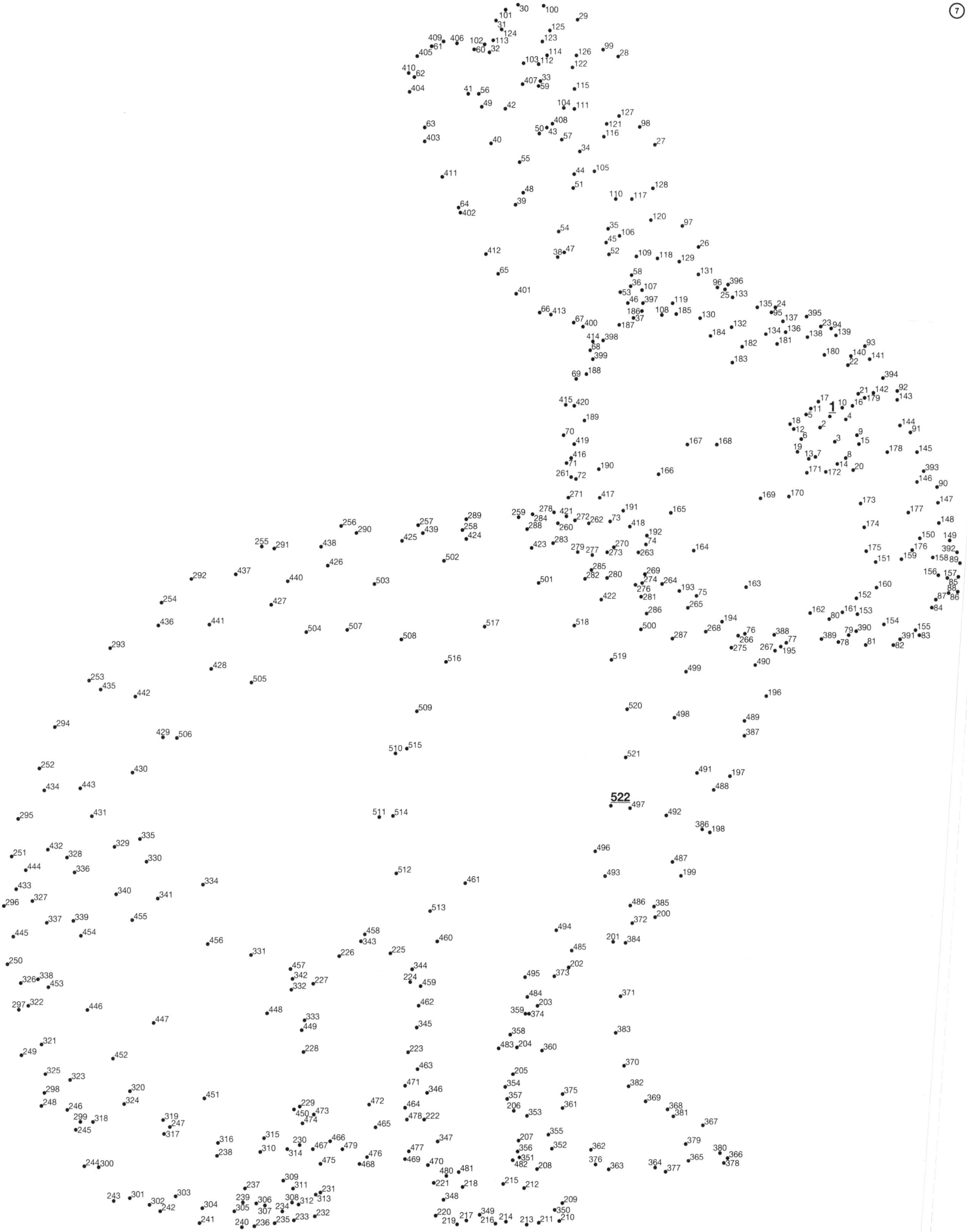

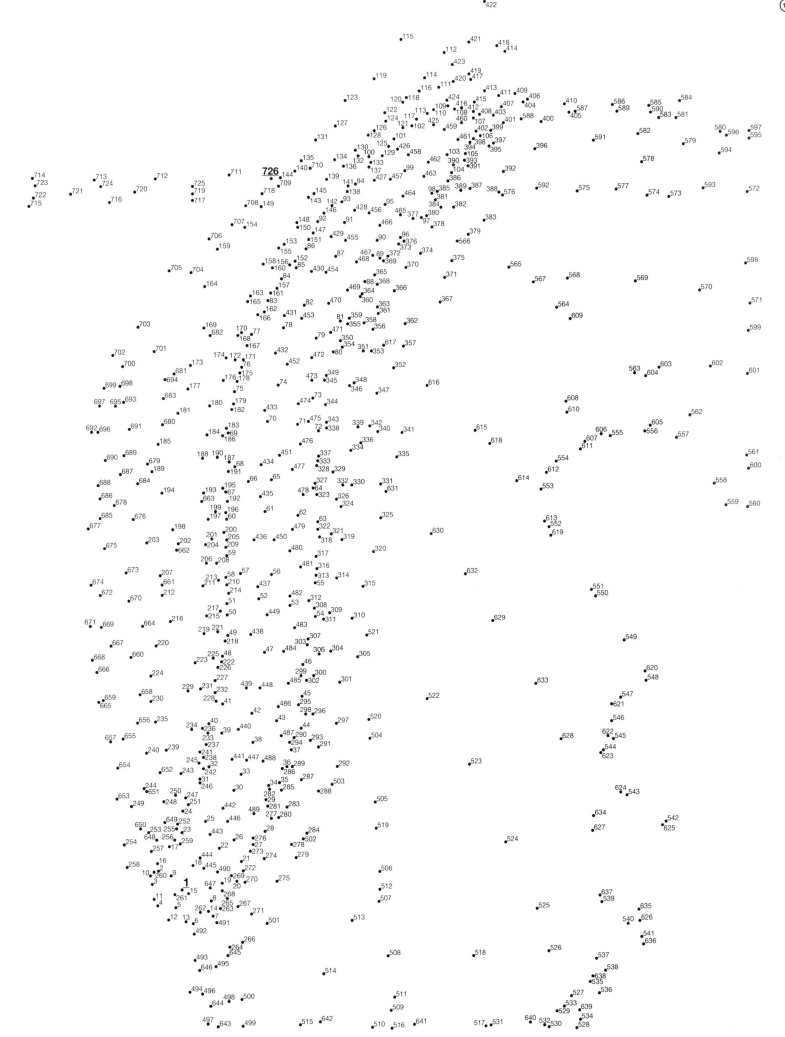

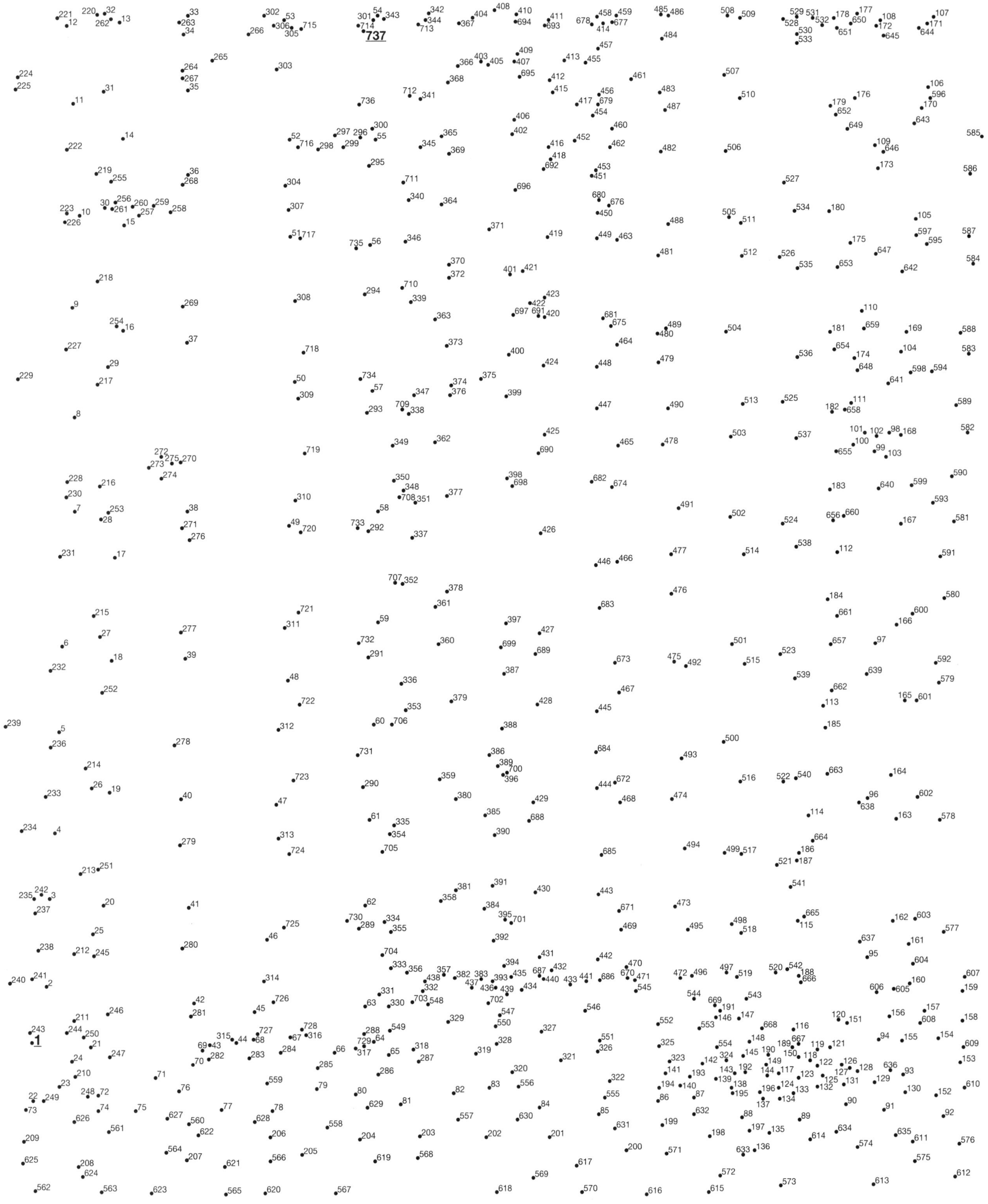

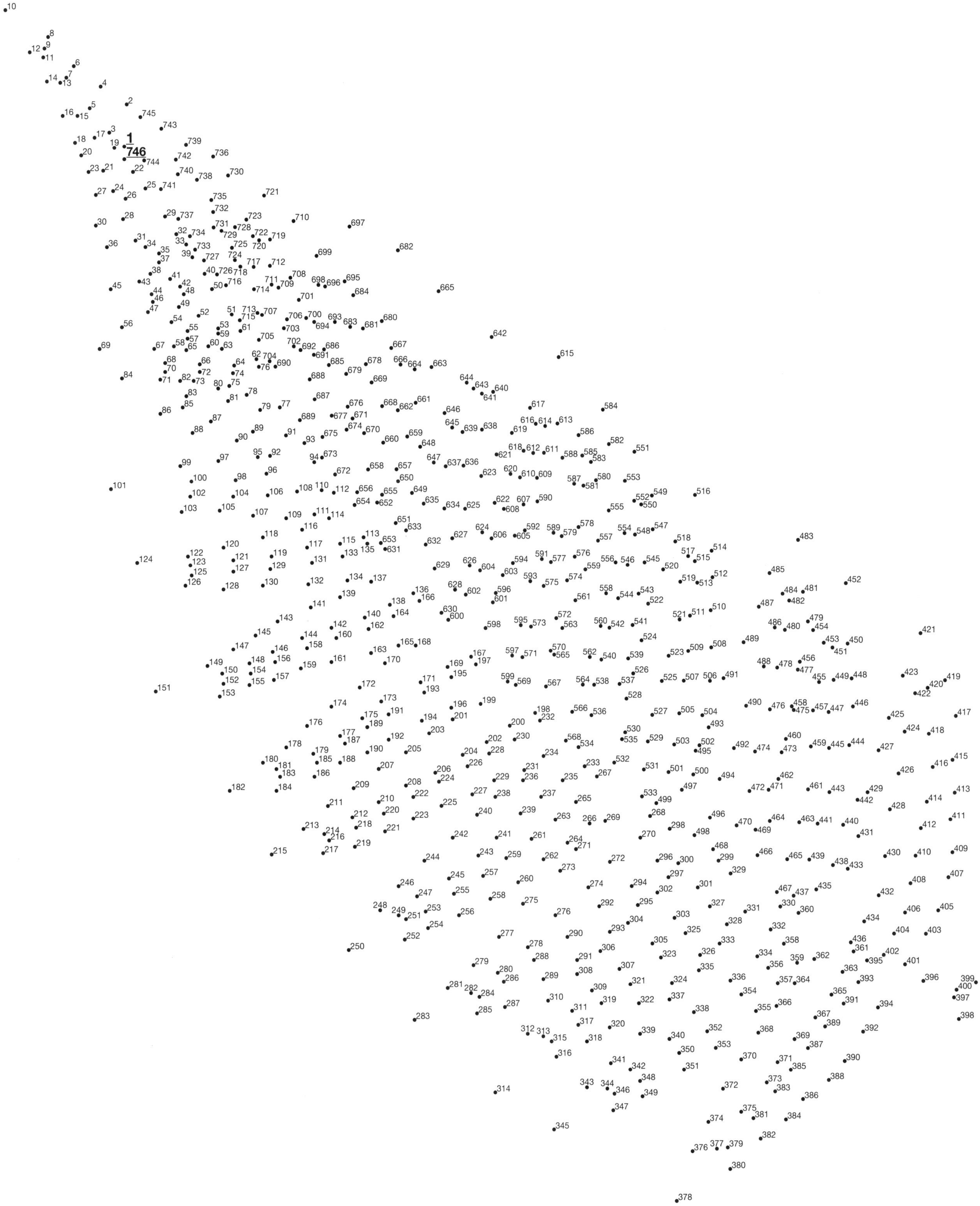

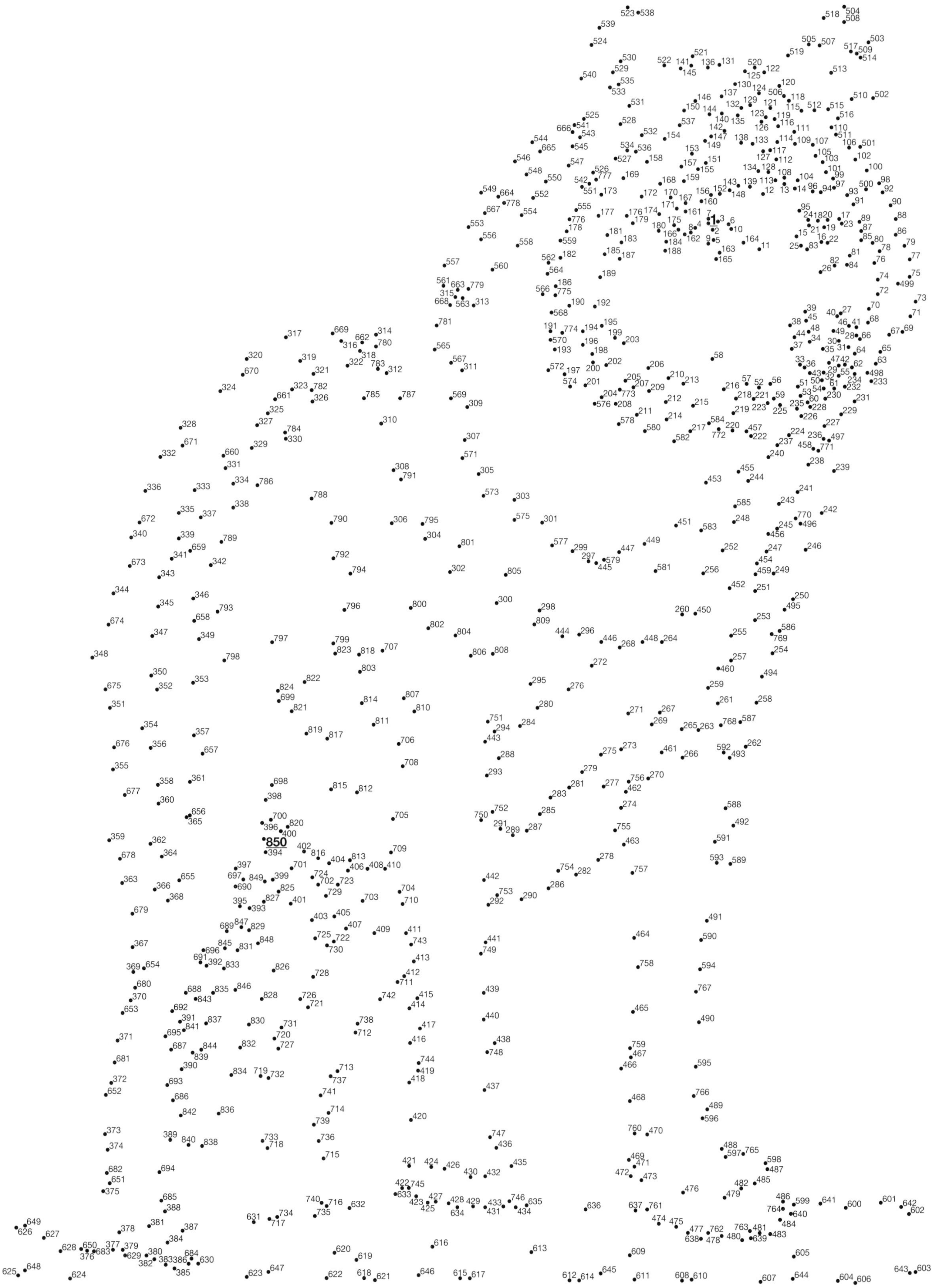

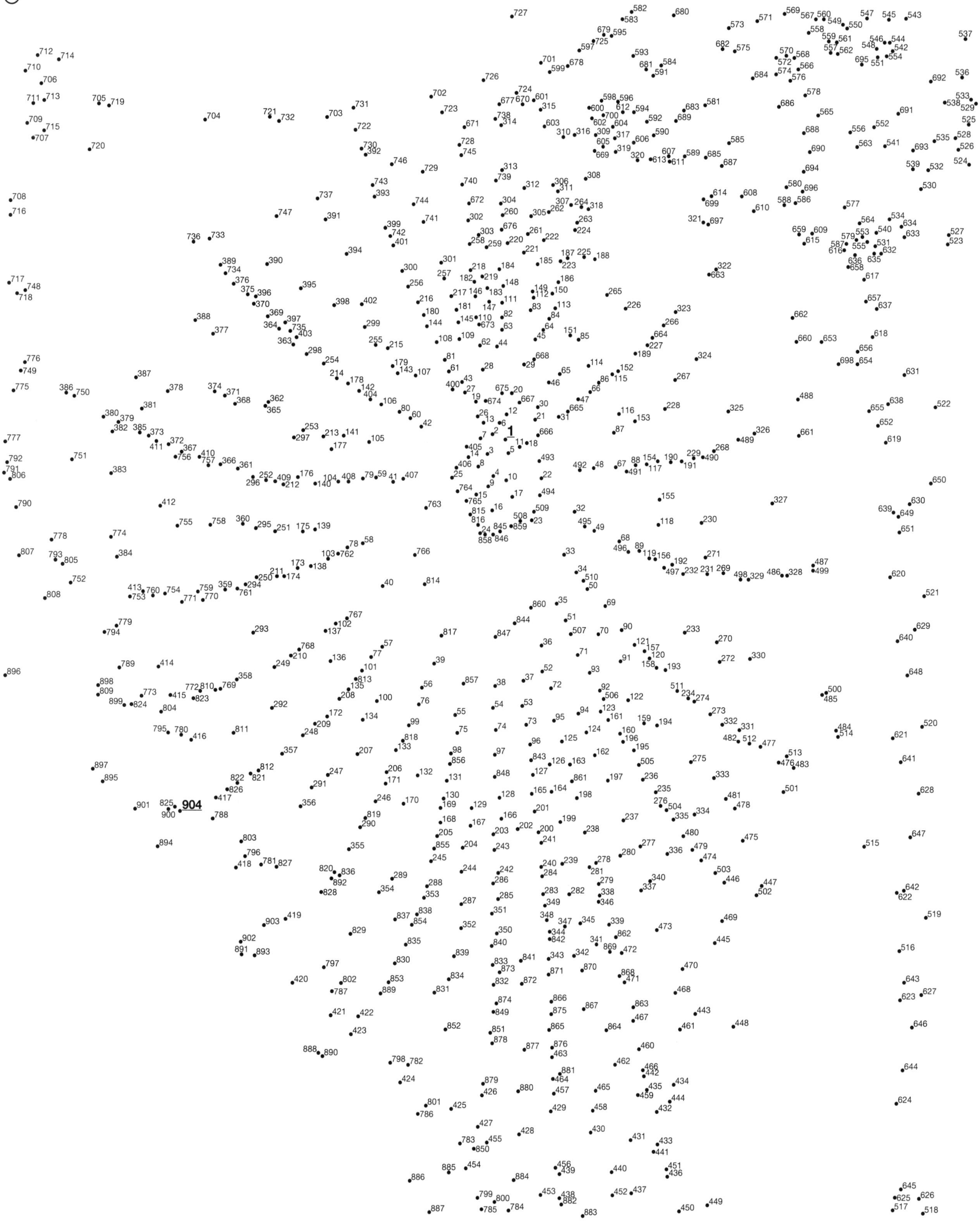

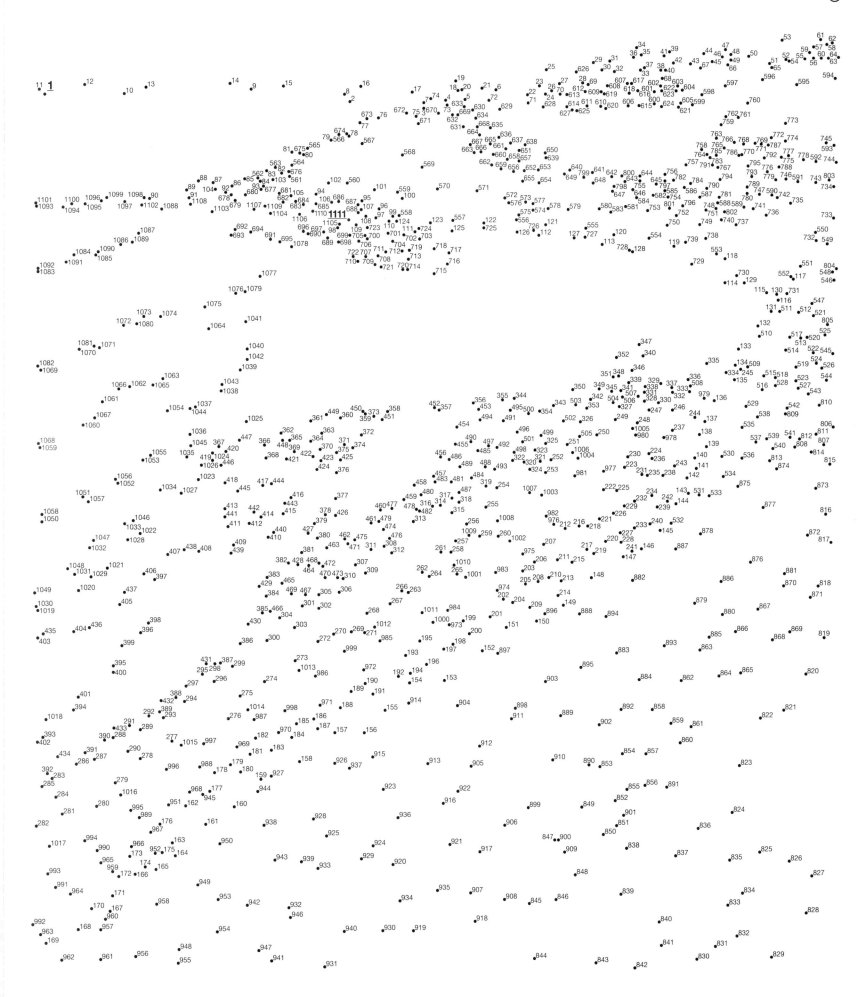

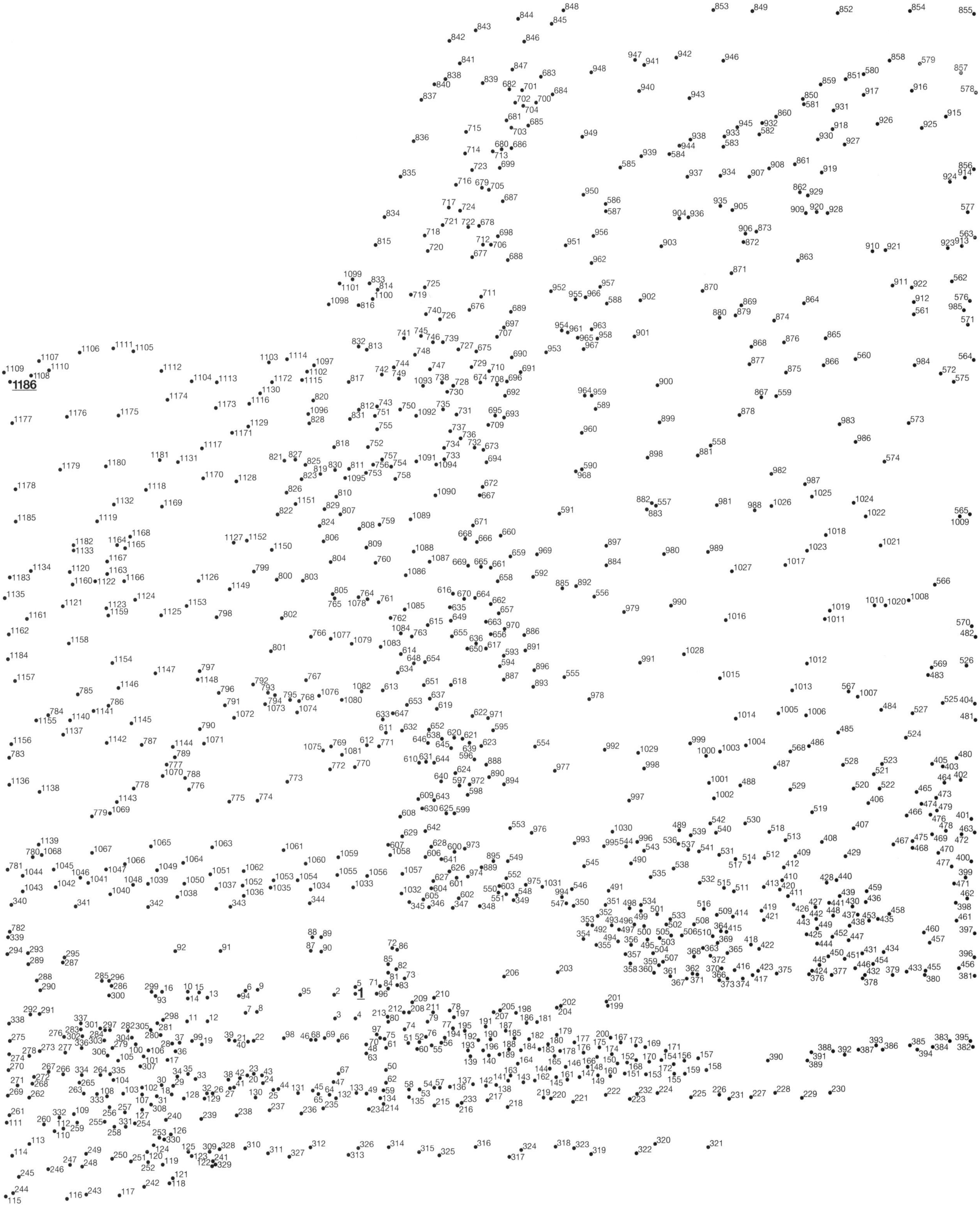

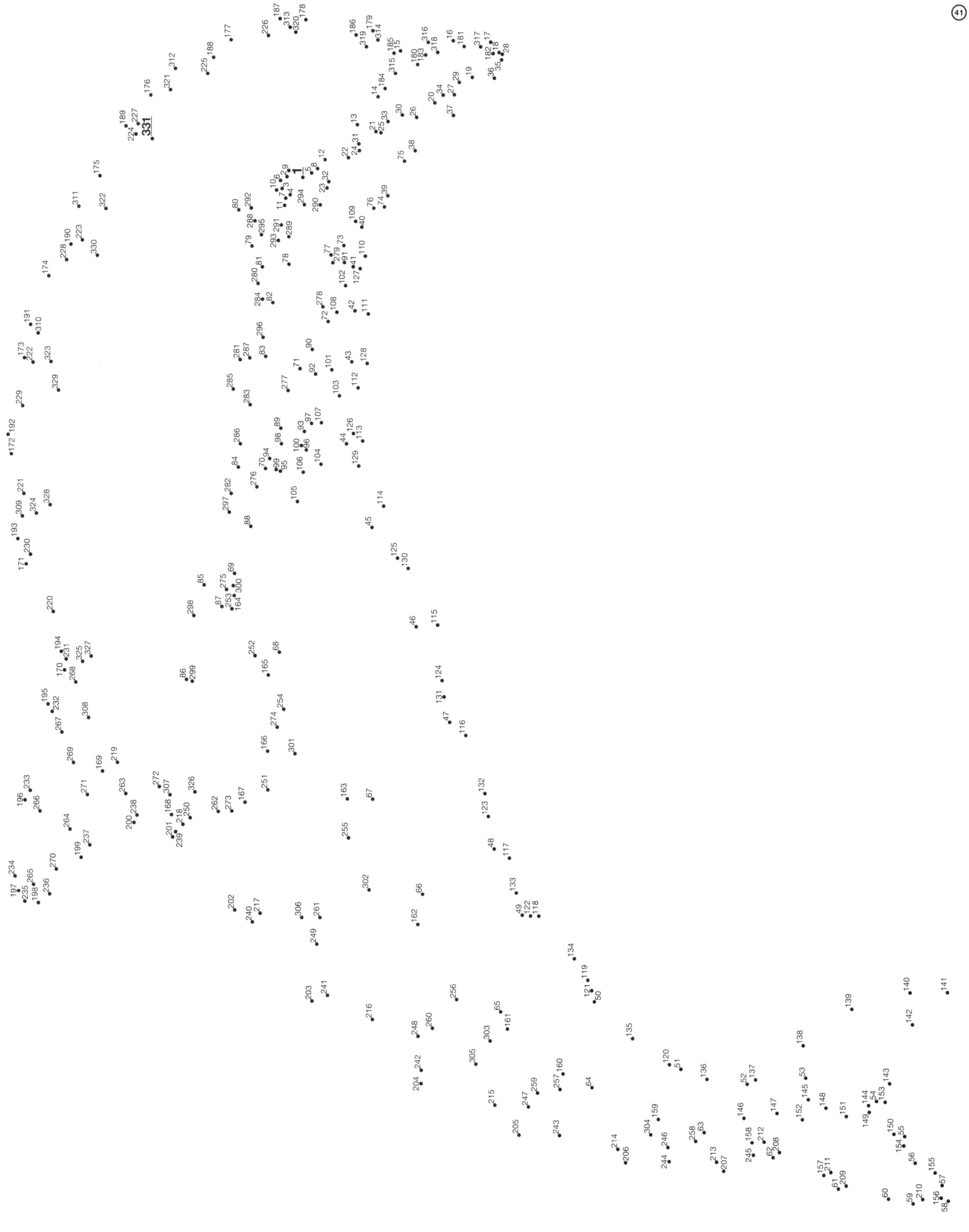

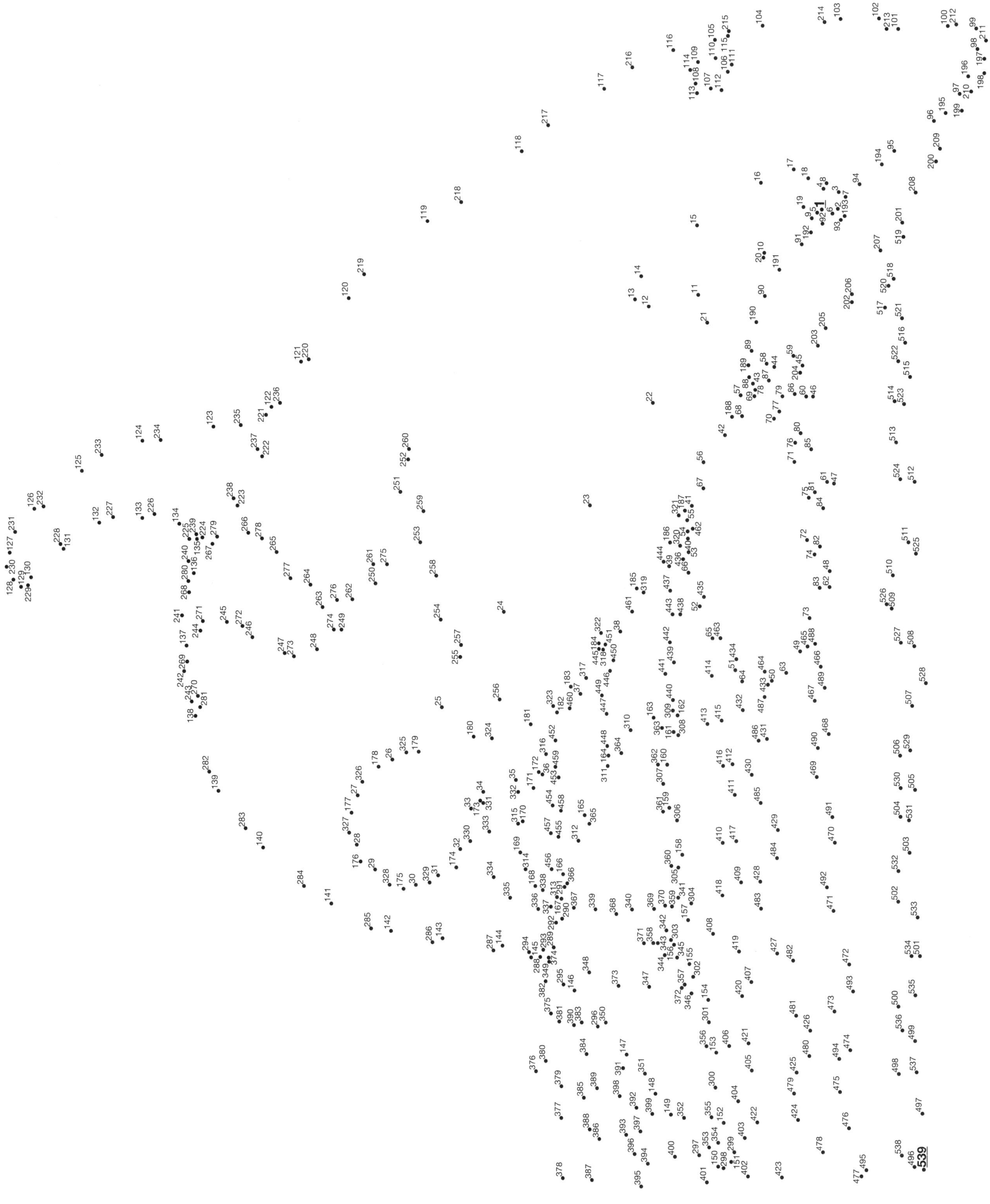

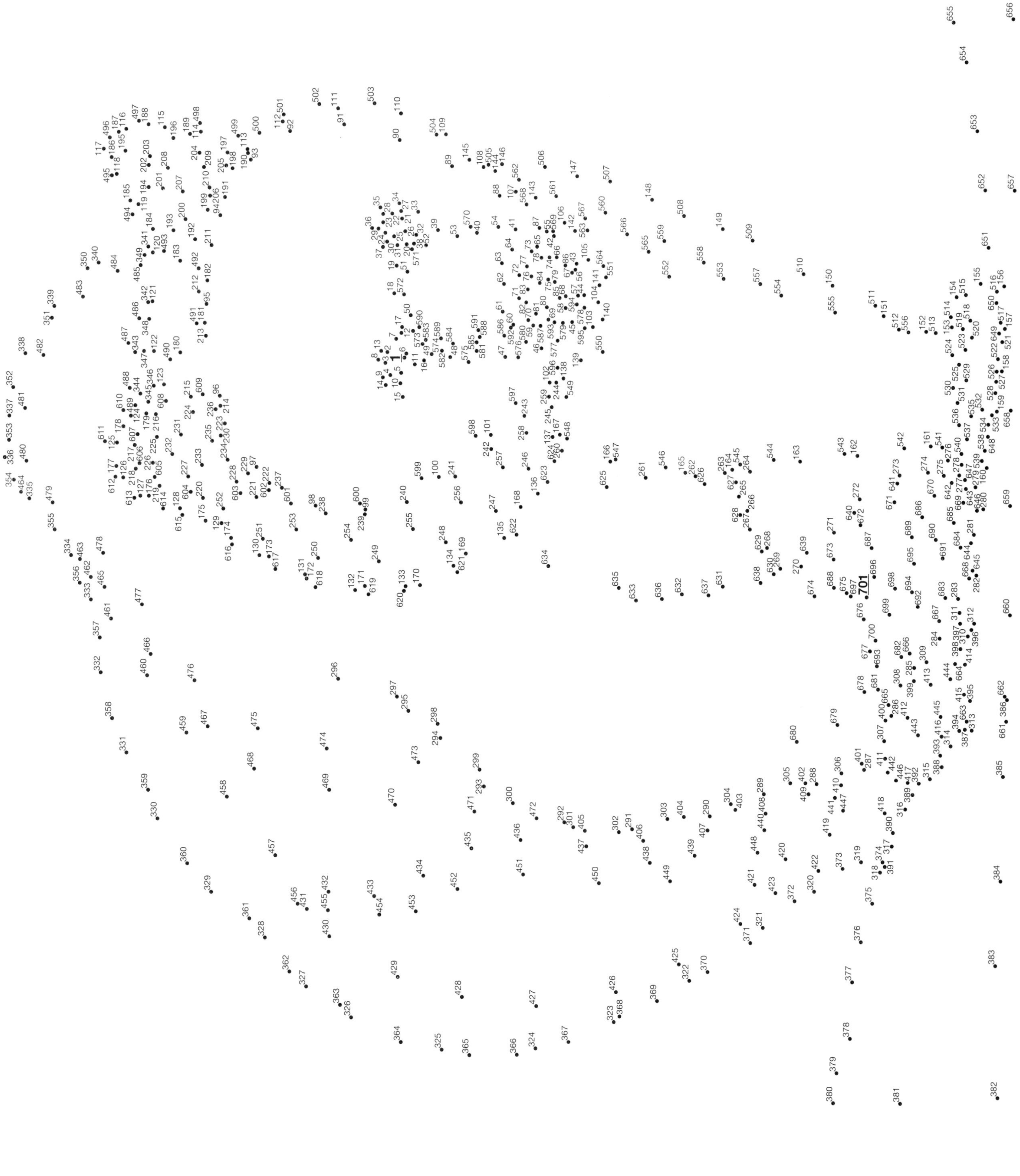

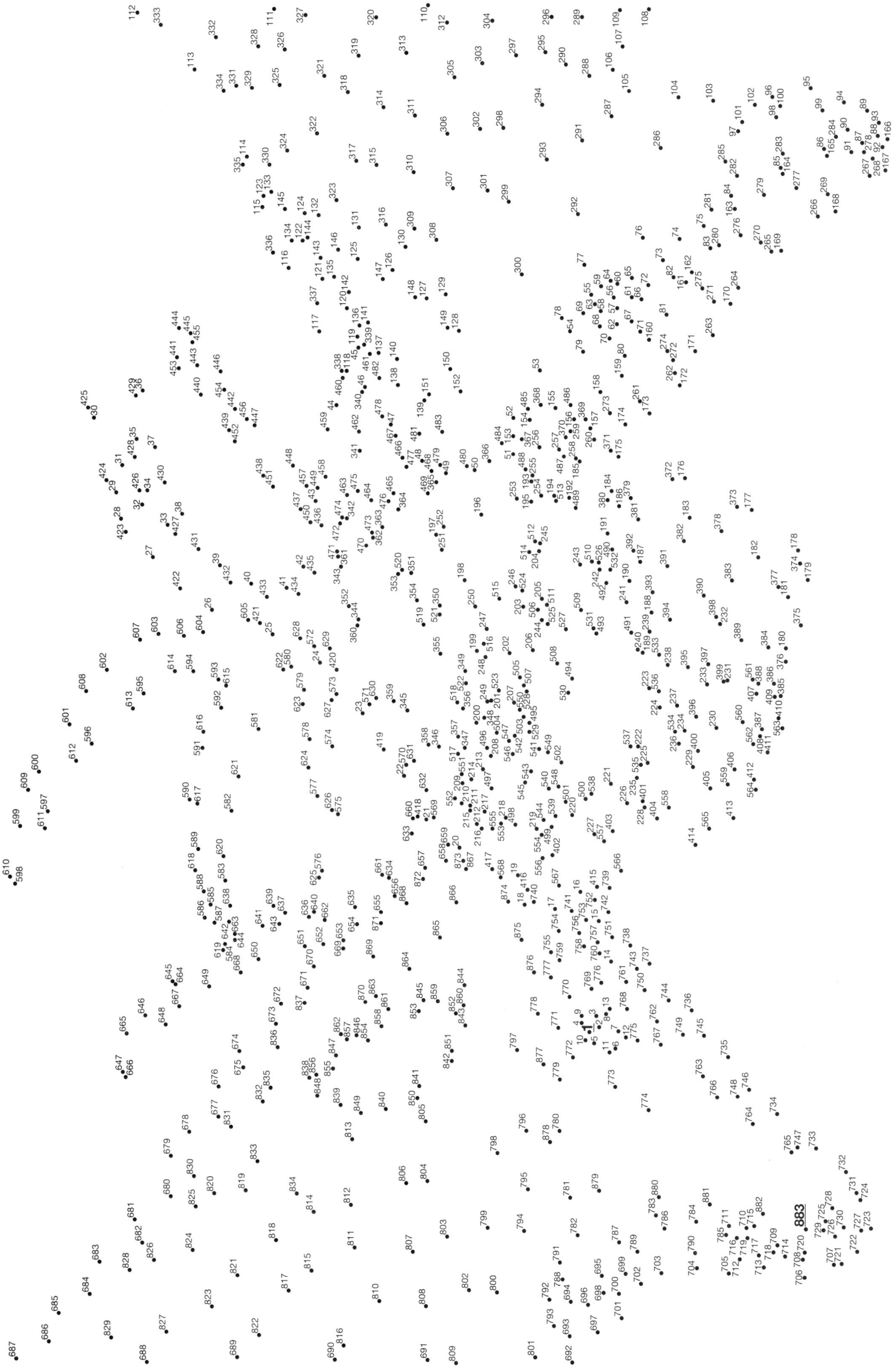

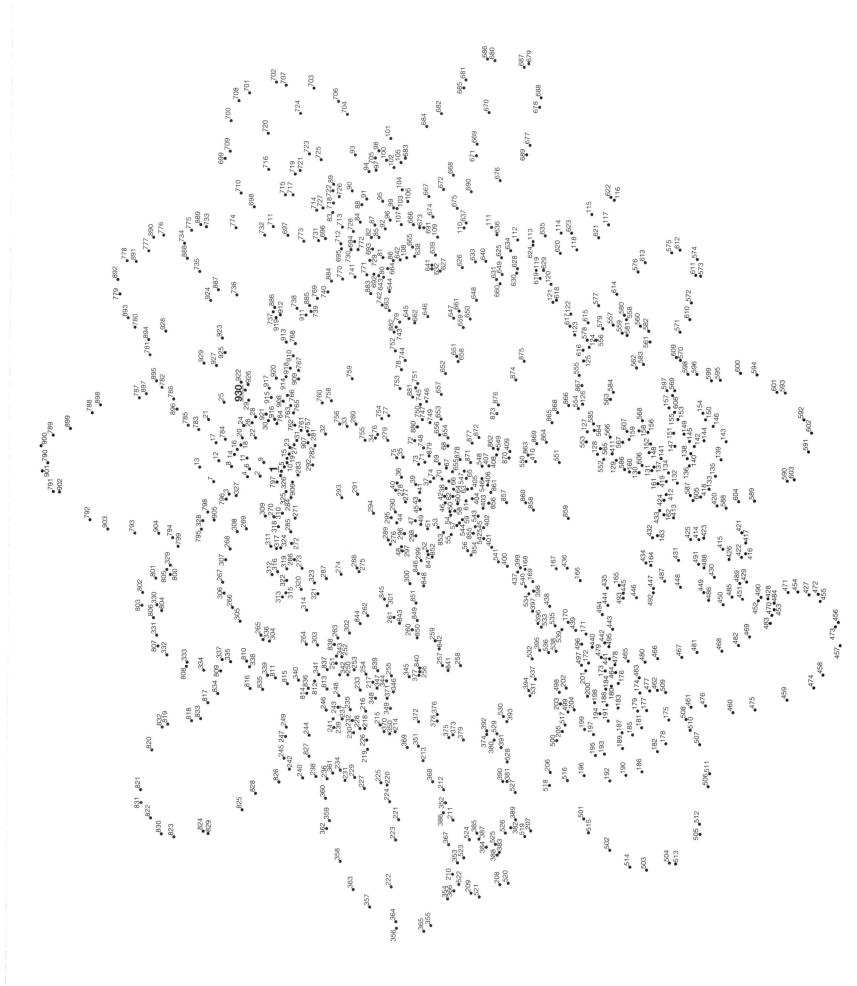

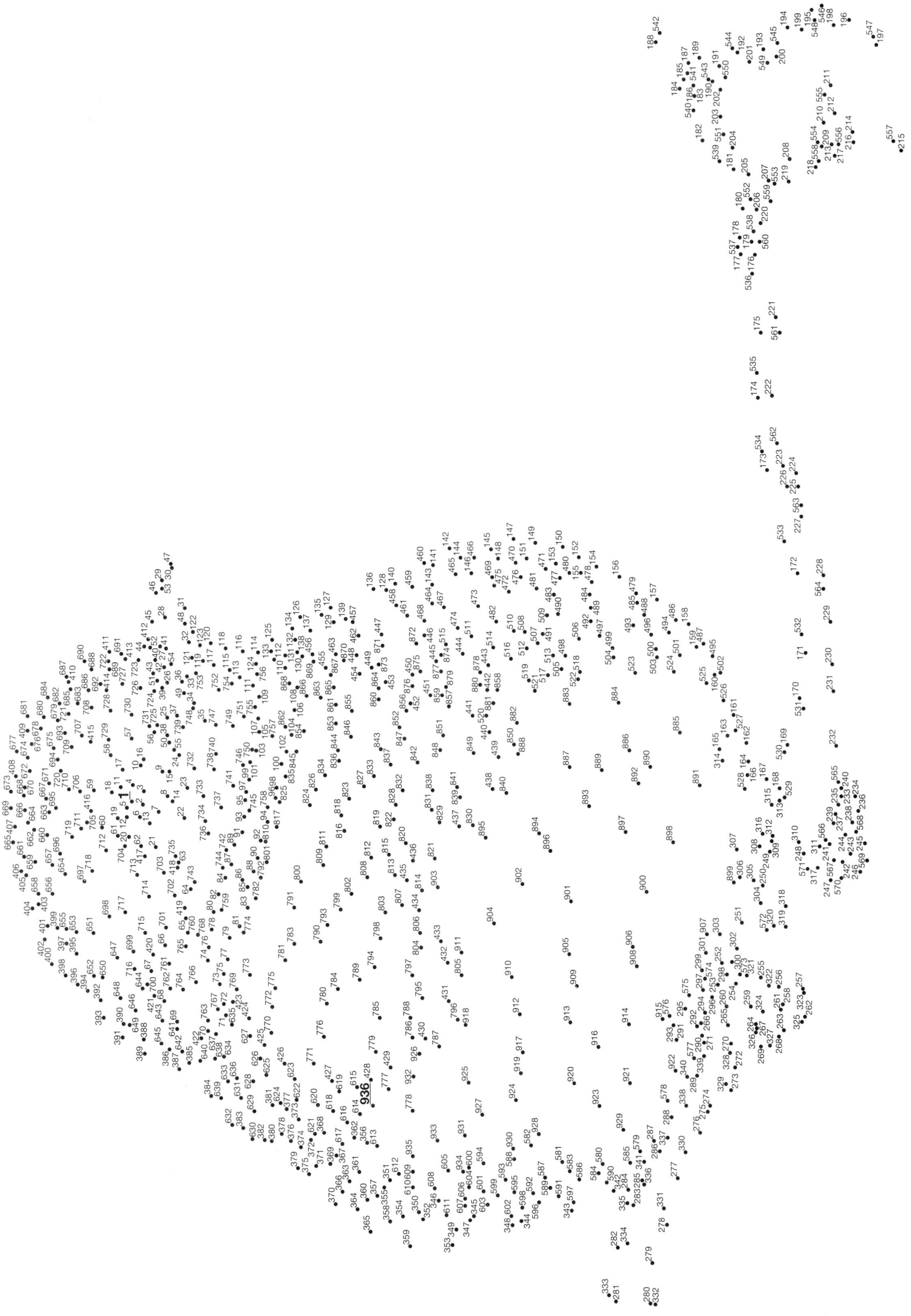

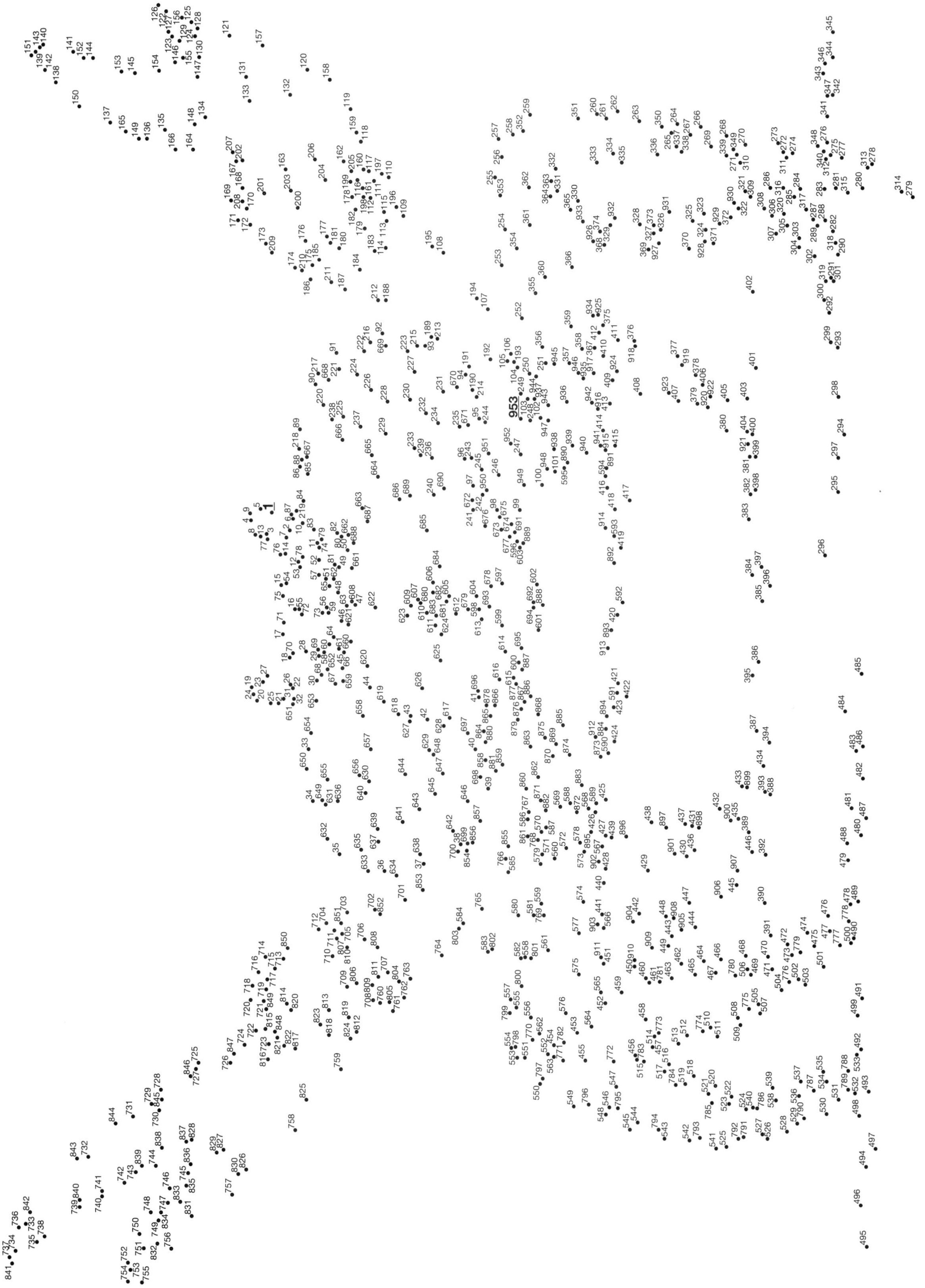

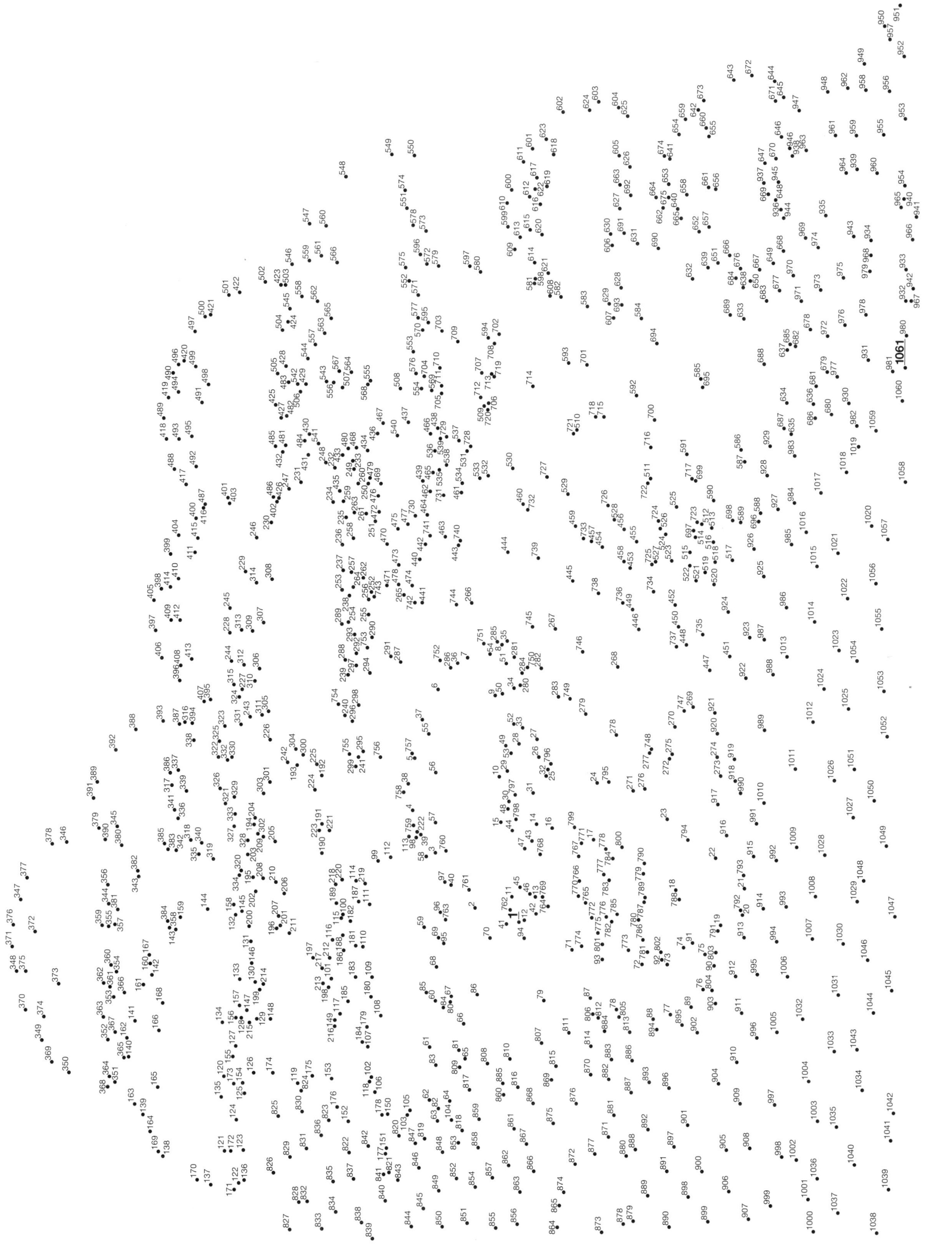

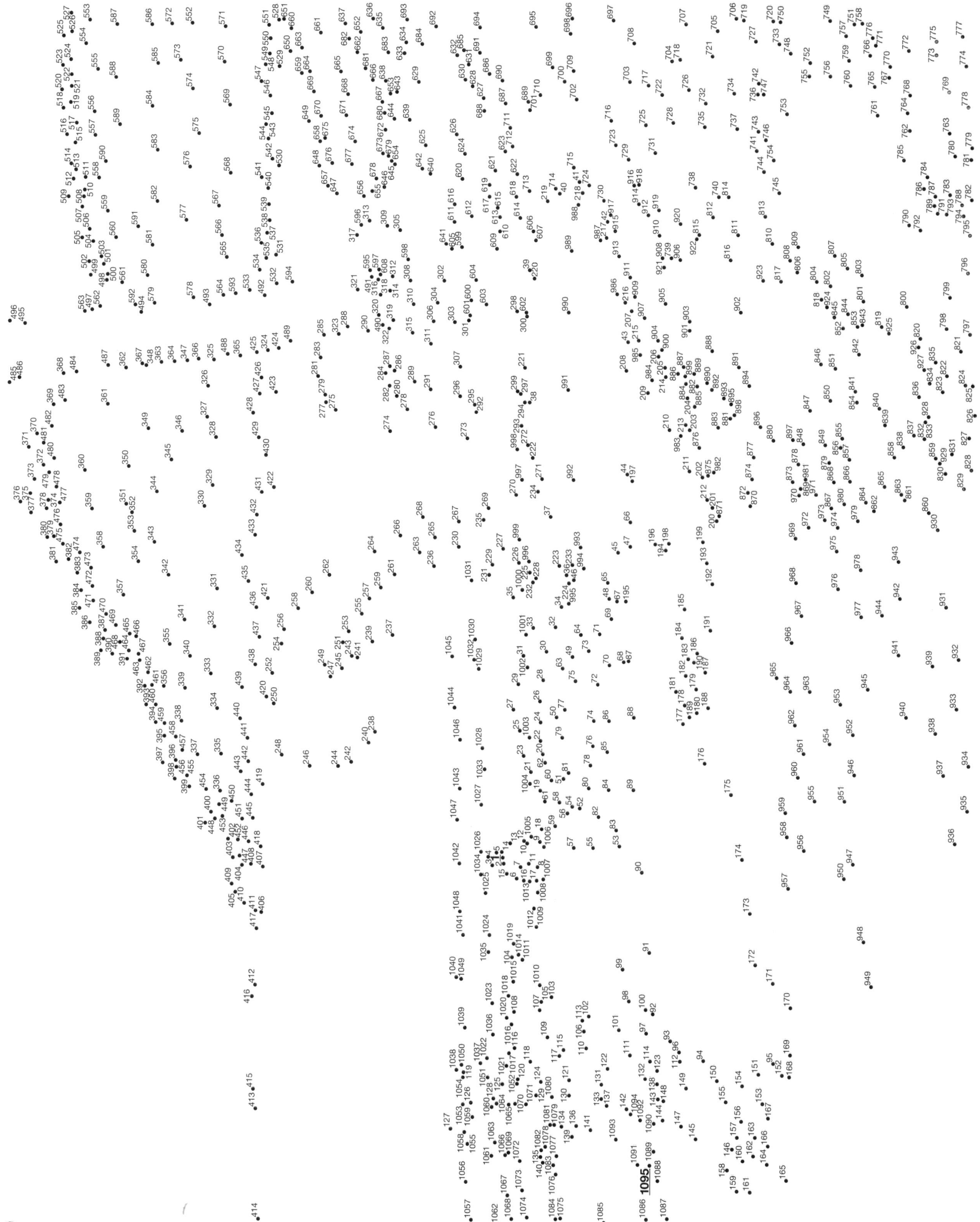

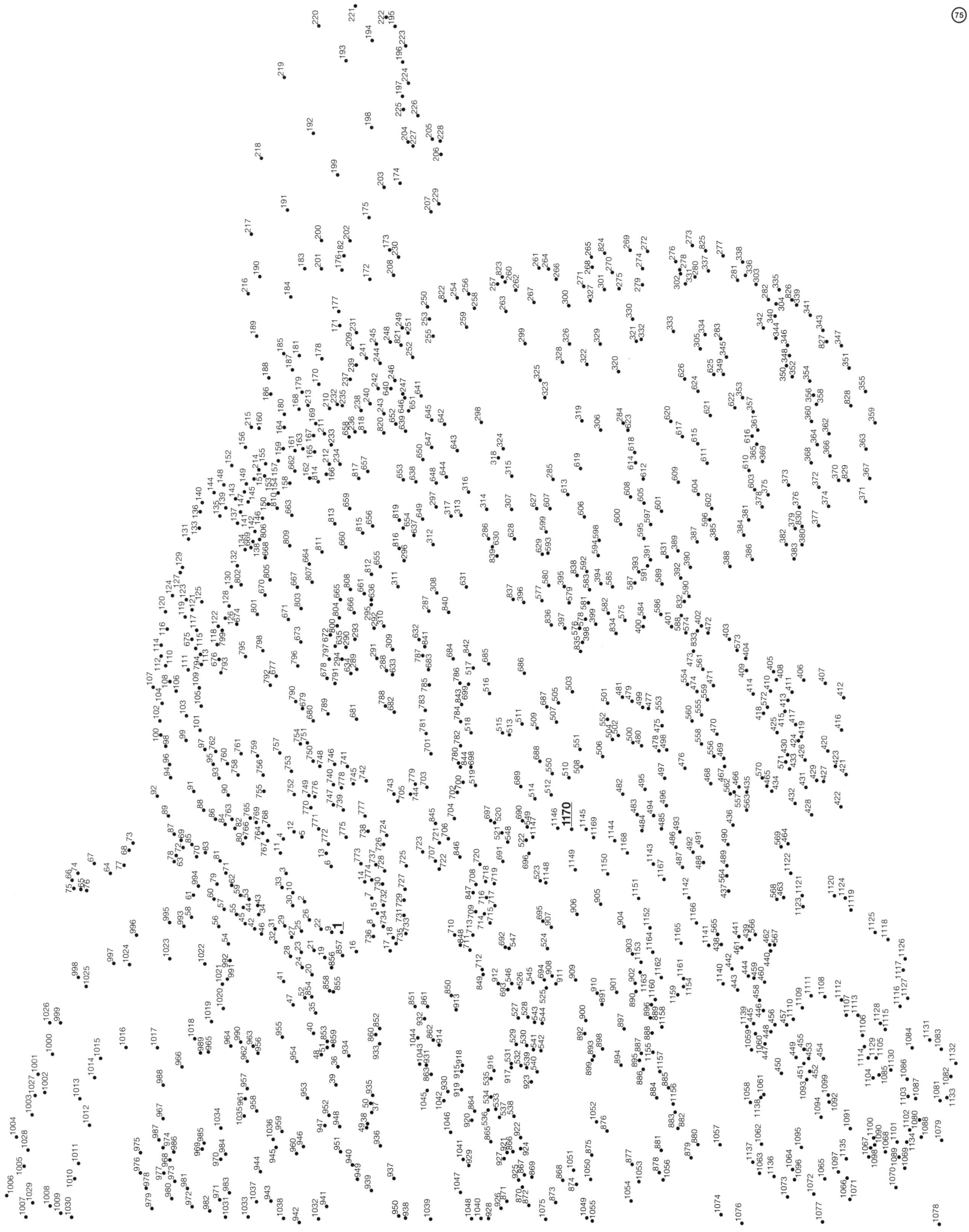

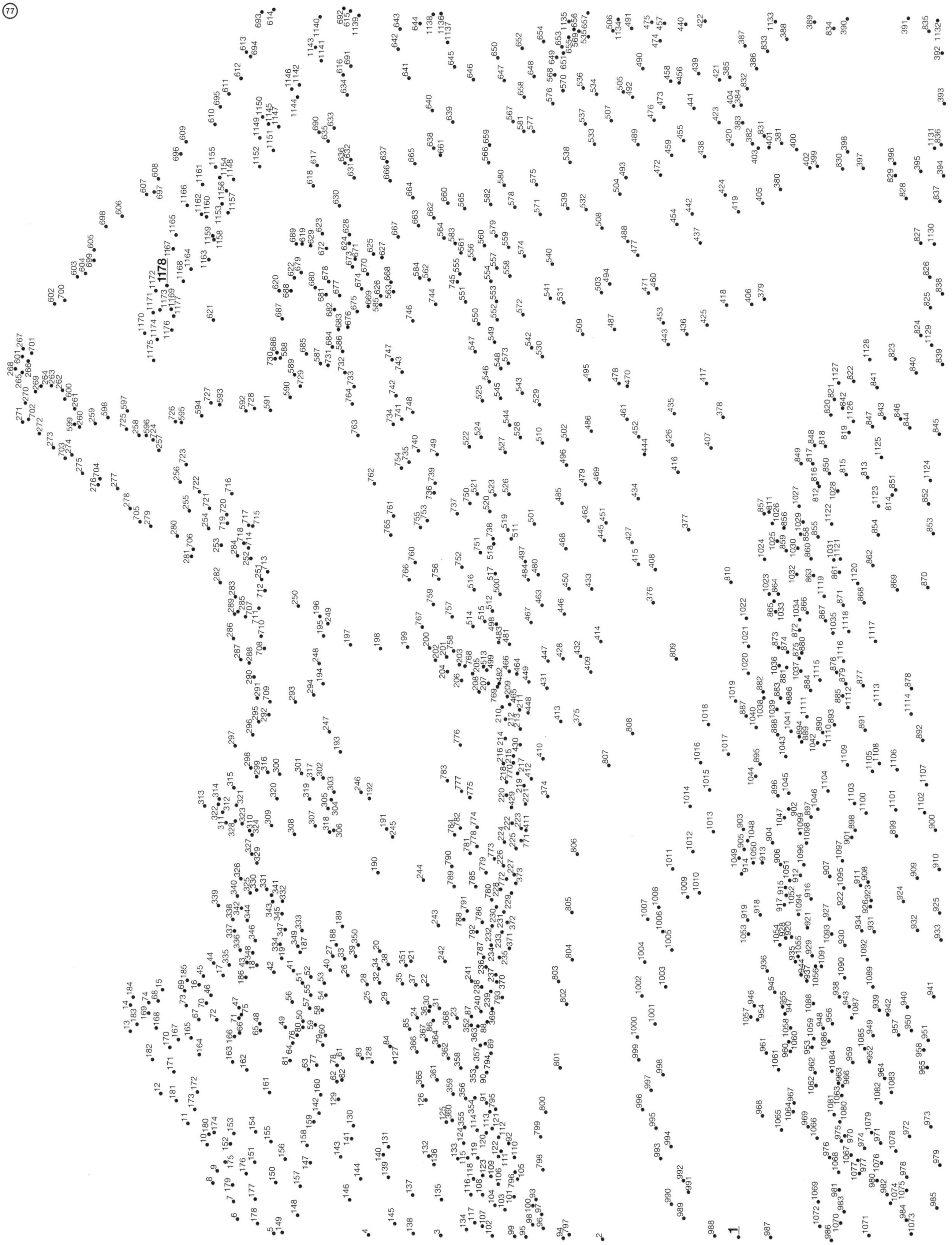

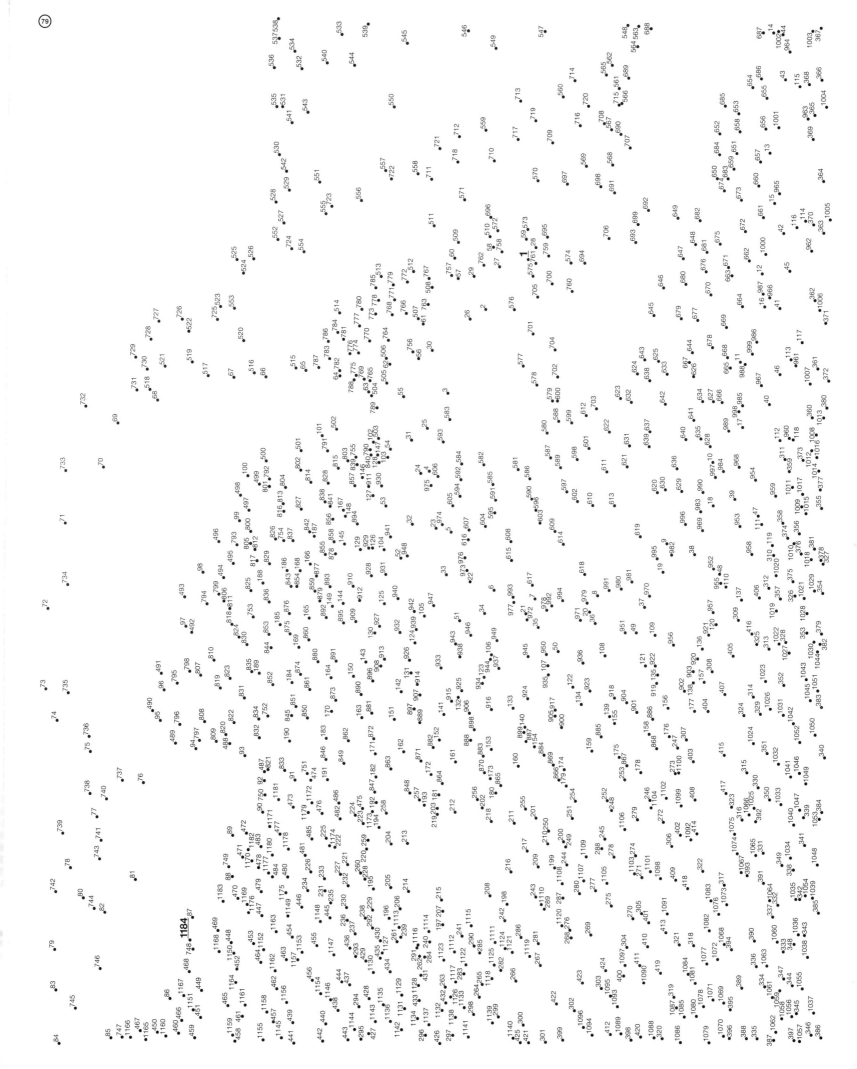

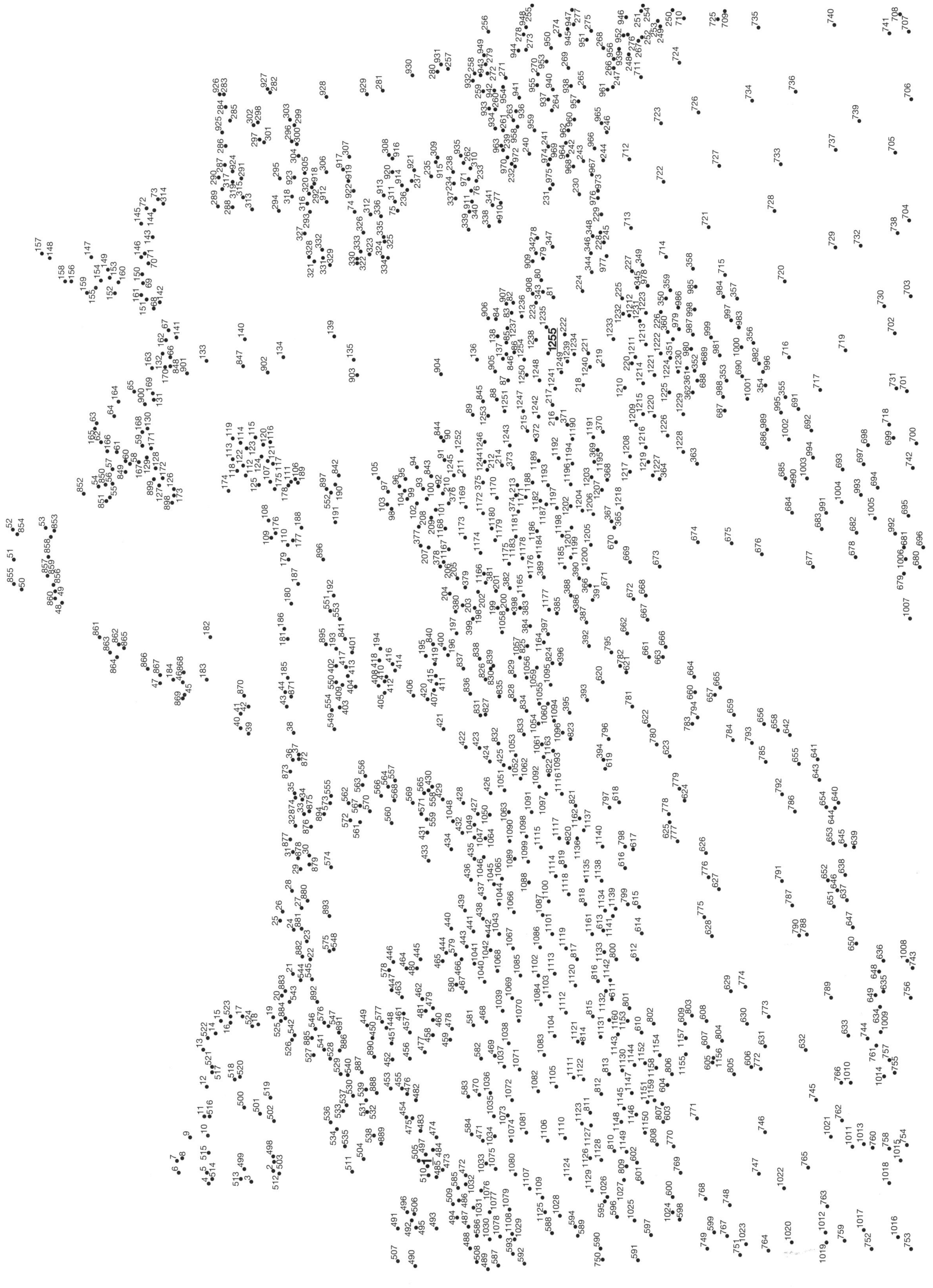

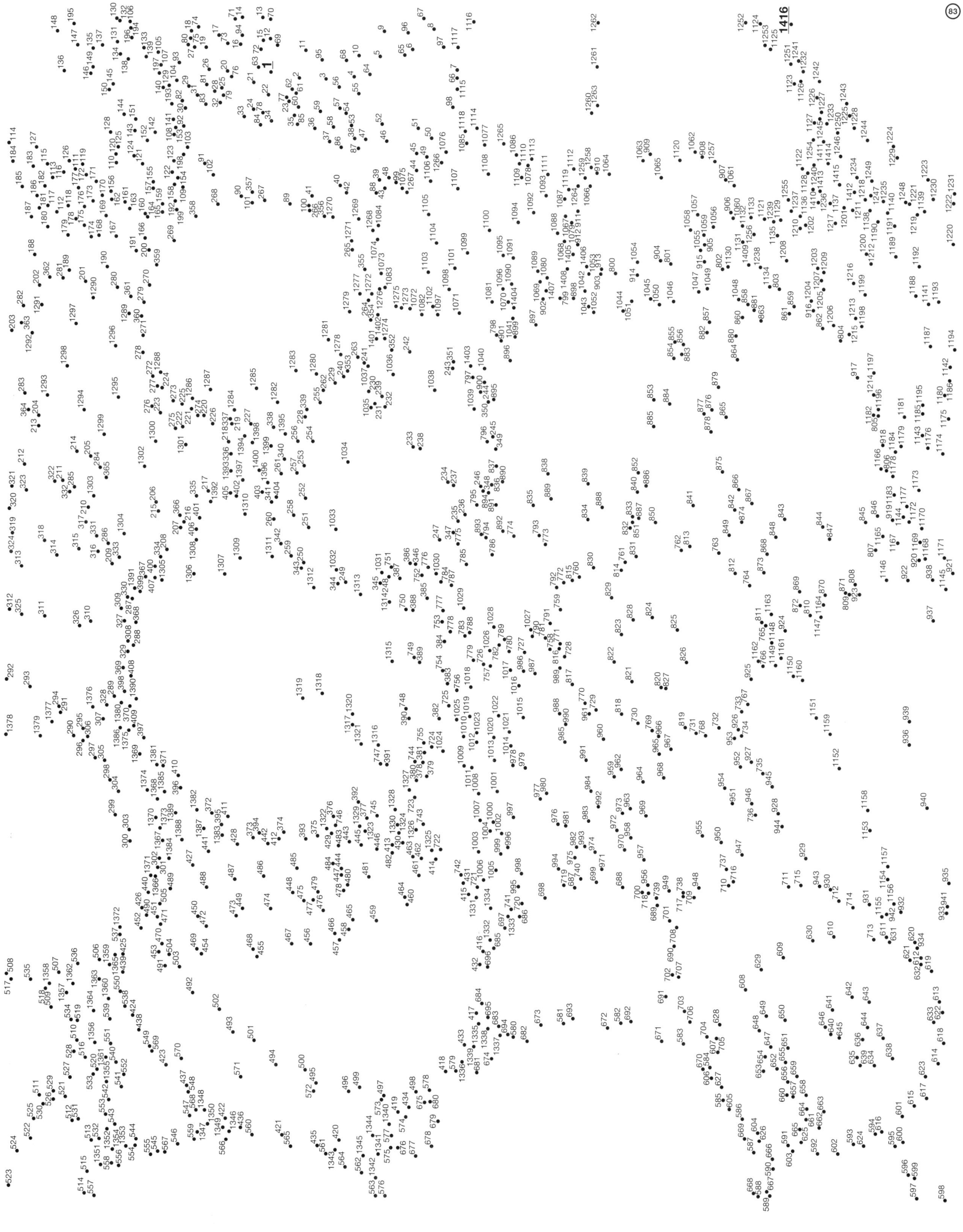

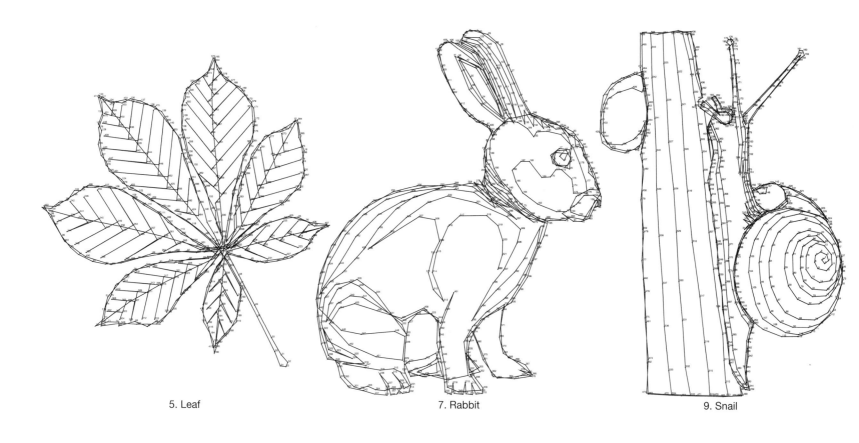

5. Leaf

7. Rabbit

9. Snail

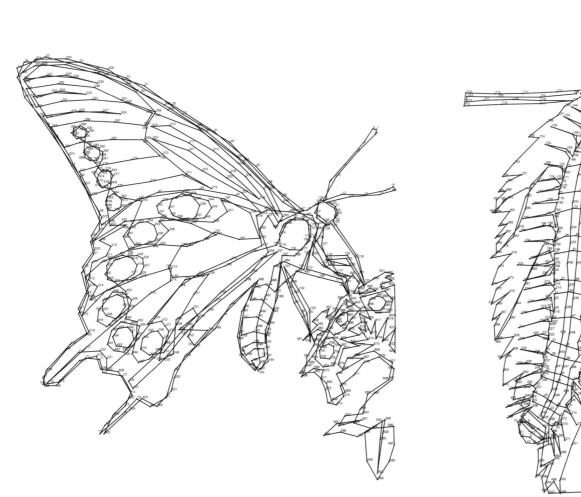

11. Butterfly

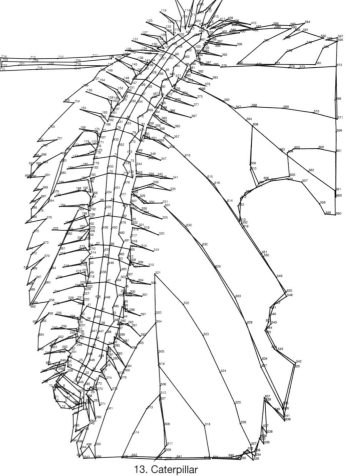

13. Caterpillar

15. Woodland

17. Fern

19. Wolf

21. Gooseberries

23 Horse

25. Spider's web

27. Penguins

29. Bird in flight

31. Owl

33. Fox

35. Coastal inlet

37. Cabin, lake and cliff

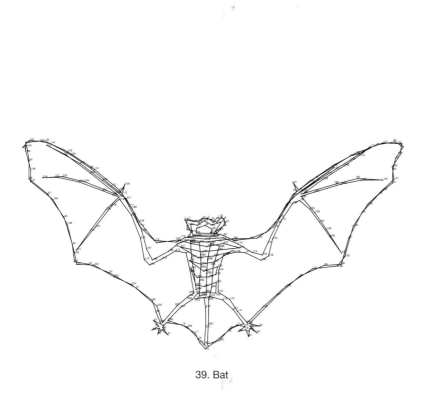

39. Bat

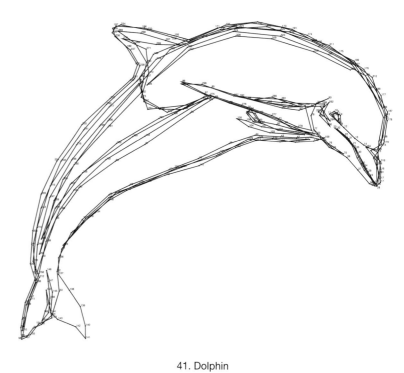

41. Dolphin

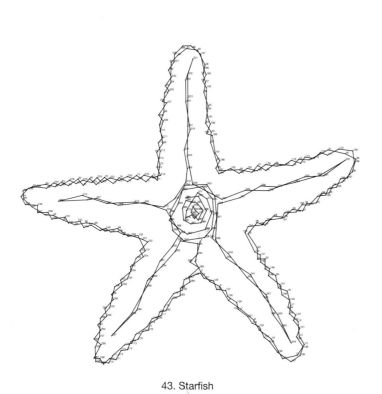

43. Starfish

45. Whale

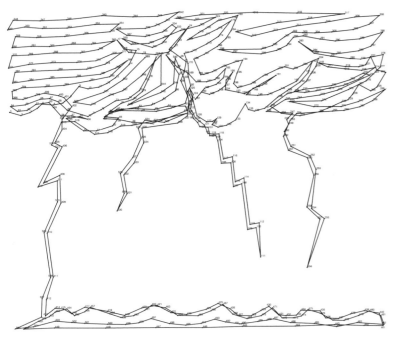

47. Storm

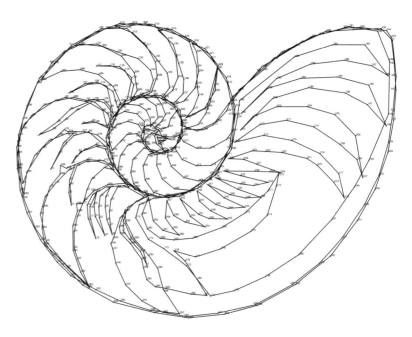

49. Shell

51. Grizzly bear

53. Squirrel

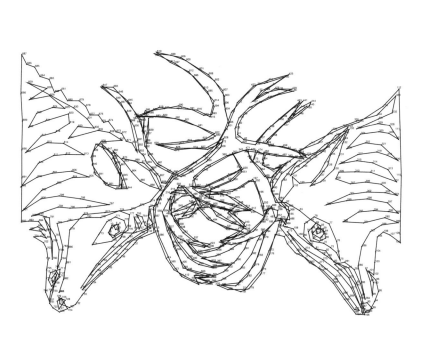

55. Stags

57. Blossom

59. Robin

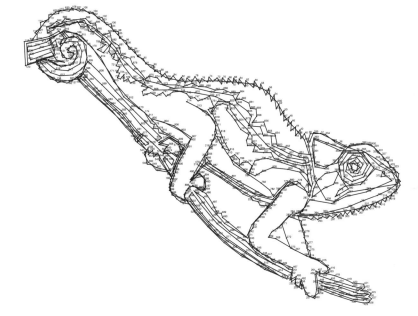

61. Chameleon

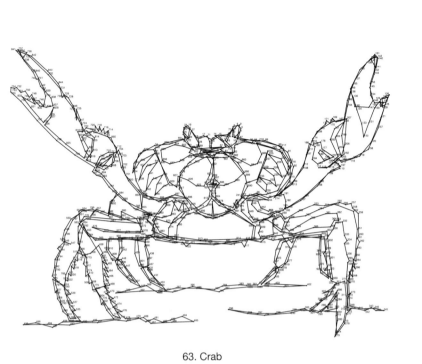

63. Crab

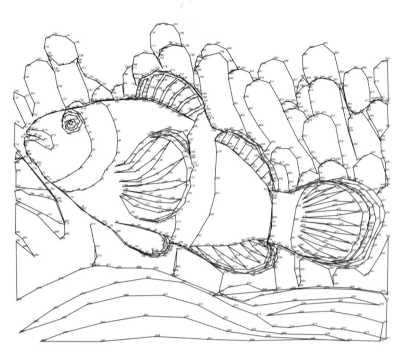

65. Clownfish

67. Mushrooms

69. Tropical beach

71. Frog

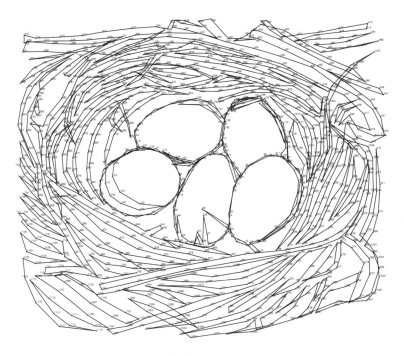

73. Bird's nest

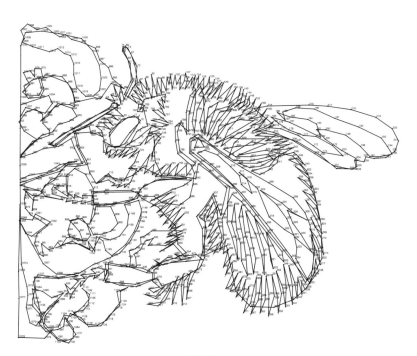

75. Bee

77. Mountain scene

79. Crashing wave

81. Cliff-edge ruins

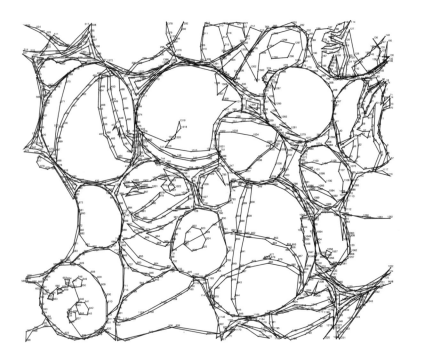

83. Pebbles

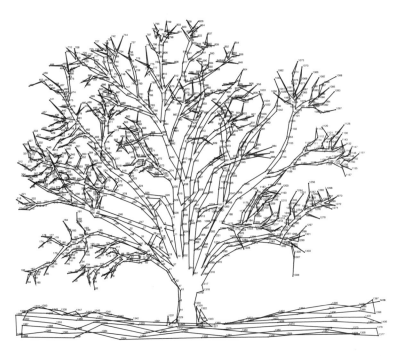

85. Winter tree